JUNK SHOP HEART

KIRK DIEDRICH

For Maria

Matia mou

I write because she exists.

BEGINNING

A brunette with a guarded heart and dangerous curves will be the sweet, slow death of me; as bees in honey drown.

CREATE

I create word pictures from my experiences filtered through my heart and mind.

I bleed this ink in hopes that others will read it and connect in a way that makes them feel something, anything. I want to affect the rate of their heartbeat, the pupils of their eyes, the breath in their lungs.

Because that's what happened to me when I saw her eyes, felt her skin and tasted her.

I want to create something that captures the moments in the amber of my words so people know there was a perfect storm of us and it was lightning in her eyes and thunder in my heart and a rain of beauty that drenched our souls to the bone.

FATE

Hearts entwined, the roots
going deep
into the past
where Fate
touched them
and said, "Yes. These two here."

WORDS LIKE ARMS

Let my words
hold you
until
my arms
finally can.

THROUGH THE LEAVES

Thoughts of her sough
through me
leaves
caught
in the breeze
dancing
in the air
of her
thick with the scent
of cherry blossoms.

UNEARTHED

She's unearthed words
buried deep inside me
where I kept them
hidden
with my hope.

A Laugh Like Fingertips

Her laugh runs barefoot
through my head;
fingertips trailing lazily
against the walls,
determined
to leave
a trace of her
behind.

SAFE WORDS

Fall.
My words
will guide you
softly
down into
the safety
of my arms.

JUNK SHOP HEART

My heart isn't Tiffany.
It's made of broken dreams
strung together with hope.
But, it sings her name
from the bottom
of my junk shop heart.

FAERIETALE ENDING

Once upon a time
a girl in a tower
rescued a knight
from his own dragon.
She let down her guard
so he could climb
to safety
in her heart.

DANGER: HEARTS

Love should be dangerous.
Crush hearts.
Play with the speed of blood
in veins.
Bleed your souls out.
Love fiercely.
Because all of this ends.

Fall.

Now.

SMOKE

She consumes me
like a bright fire
burning deep
within my ribs.
I breathe flame,
sigh smoke.
I choke
on the heady fumes
of her beauty.

SAFE HARBOR

Moor my rudderless boat
on your soft shore
until the storm passes.
Help repair the damage.
Paint your name on me,
I'll sail you anywhere.

NIGHT FOR DAY

In dreams
I hold her
all night long.

Awake,
I dream her,
curse the dawn.

MEROPE

The bright flecks
in her dark eyes
are the whirling stars
in my only sky.

SHE'S THUNDERSTORMS

She is a Summer thunderstorm inside me,
my heart's fierce rumble,
lightning forks across my skin.

Her beauty is a deluge
washing my soul.

BOOKENDS

I go to sleep
thinking of her.

I wake
thinking of her.

She is both
the bookends
and the stories between.

THAT KISS

The transcendent kiss
that burns intense,
scars your psyche;
a ghost in the halls of your head
that refuses to fade.

Come.

Kiss me that way.

O, For a Muse

Fall for
an artist,
writer,
poet
and prepare to be
their muse,
their words,
their subject,
their page,
their canvas,
their obsession,
theirs.

ABSOLUTELY

All I want to do
is absolutely everything
and absolutely nothing
with you
for as long
as my heart beats.

BLIND GIRL

I wish for once
that she could see
the her that I can see;
beauty that both
steals my breath
and gives it back to me.

THE HEART OF A MUSE

How do you win
the heart of a Muse?
Be her own soul's mirror.
Reflect back
her beauty,
so she folds
her wings,
kneels
and listens
to your love song of her.

WORTH

She looks at me
like there's something there.

Worth seeing.

Worth knowing.

Worth keeping.

CAREFREE GIRL

She laughs
and in that moment
I glimpse
the young girl
who dreamt of
carefree nights
in safe arms
wrapped around her
like a favorite shirt.

SECRET POOL

I see the you
the one kept
hidden
in plain sight
needs
desires
longing
play upon your face;
reflections
from the water
where I'd gladly drown.

THREE THINGS I KNOW

I just woke up one day and found her lying there in my heart.

She is every good childhood memory happening at once.

Each story she shares makes me want to be in the rest of them.

HER HOME IN MY HEART

She swept
cobwebs from corners,
dust from the floors.
Shook out the rugs
and bolted the door.
Her home in my heart
shines as never before.

THE MUSIC OF US

A heavy hush
shakes the air
between us.
Our sighs,
a splendid music
of thought suspended.
My eyes, ears listen
for her breath to change.
Enfolding her in my arms,
quiet and close enough
for our hearts,
our lungs,
our rhythms to sync.
In stillness,
we become one.
We become us.

She

She has the kind of beauty that shames your understanding of the word.

She is the waking dream I've had for so long.

She is the deep ache I couldn't put a face to or a finger on.

She smiles and steals my breath like a thief.

She makes me keenly aware that I have a heart.

EVERYTHOUGHT

You are not
an afterthought.

You are
an everythought.

THIEF

You found me
when I wasn't looking.

You unlocked my heart
with a key I didn't know existed.

You stole it
like it was yours to begin with.

Love Past the Past

I will love you
past your doubts
if you can love me
past my faults.

KINTSUKUROI HEART

Find your Muse.

Let her pour her beauty as gold into the cracks of your heart.

Return it in a storm of words that raises the beat of hers.

DANCE

Let me lead.
I will dance you
to the edge of ecstasy,
breathless,
lingering there
until the song ends
and you let go
knowing
I've got you.

Lullaby

To feel her
nestled in my arms,
head on my chest
listening
to the heart she owns
whisper her to sleep
with the lullaby
of her own name.

PHOENIX

Sparks of mischief
in your eyes.
You look like
the best kind of trouble.
Let's burn our past down
and make something better
from its ashes.

DANGEROUS

Kissing her
is warm wet
dangerous magic.
Her mouth
conjures
a storm
inside me.
I am bewitched
by the lightning
crackling
between us
and the thunder
of our heartbeats.

USED HEART

She drew my used heart
from a box of junk,
blew the dust from it,
turned it in her hands
and said,
"I think I can do something with this."

WILD HAIRED GIRL

My wild haired girl,
black fire for a mane.
Medusa incarnate.
Erato unchained.
Eyes like a snakebite
straight to the vein;
races my heart,
drives me insane.

NEW WORDS

She shimmers in the dark,
glowing from within.
Music fills my ears,
she fills my hands.
So perfect we must
invent a new word
for sublime.

DISTANCE

Distance is nothing
when she is everything
Wings made of words
held aloft on hope,
miles, time vanish,
close as a touch,
soon as a heartbeat.

THIS WOMAN

Hair of black fire,
eyes of tiger jasper,
curves like
Bernini dreamed them,
smile as bright as Klieg lights.

Heroes have died for less.

Longing

I've traced
every curve
of her beautiful mind
with my thoughts, words
so she knows
the diamond sharp longing
that wracks my heart.

THE CHASE

Her heart whispered "Catch me."

His answered, "Run."

MEROPE #2

Merope
gazes
at Orion's belt
and wonders
if his hands
burn likes stars.

AUDIENCE OF ONE

All I need is
an audience
of one
to hear
my words
home
into her heart
that they
may pull aside
the curtain
of doubt
to reveal
the truth
this unperfect actor
stutters
from his
tongue-tied soul.

MIDDLE

Absence makes the heart growl, "Find her."

FIRST TASTE

Her first kiss
ruined me.
I'd gladly
spend the rest of my days
returning the favor.

TIDAL

She is the moon
that ebbs
the rushing tide
in me.
I long to
drown
in her sea
of tranquility.

The Kind of Beauty

She has the kind of beauty that takes your breath from your lungs, tears from your eyes and speeds your heart each time you look at her.

She has the kind of beauty reserved for works of art, where men spend years of their life mastering their craft to replicate.

She is beauty, stunning, transcendent, right down through to the bone, to the unfathomable depth of her heart.

She is Muse. She is wonder. She is sublime.

GIRL LIKE YOUR FAVORITE SONG

One thought.
One look.
One touch.
And, my entirety sings
this song of her.
A three-chord garage rock track,
a rough, dirty little ditty
about a girl
you can't get out of your fucking head.
Like that one song you listen to
over
and
over
and it still rips your heart out
in the best way possible.
And, when that last note sounds
you hold still,
savoring its fading echo
and then
you hit repeat.

Perfect

Black silk threads of her hair swirl like smoke on the breeze.

Her warm skin the color of a caramel crème latte glistens with condensation.

Salt air mixes with her decadent aroma.

The sea rushes to greet her running through her spread legs like a hungry lover, crash after crash after crash.

She turns and smiles, shaming the sun behind her with its brilliance.

"We should take a picture", she says, unaware that my heart already has.

HER HOME IN HIS HEAD

She haunts the hall of mirrors of his head, each flat surface reflecting back to her the beauty only he sees. Above her blaze a thousand chandeliers, every candle a remembrance of her smile. The only music arias composed to the sound of her laughter. A hearth crackles with the warmth and light of his love for her near a comfortable chair and a wall of bookshelves filled with every word she's ever inspired. This is the home he's made for her that she may never want to leave.

TO DUST

All I want is
to lie down
next to you
until
our bones
are dust.

WATER

Her dark ringlets still wet from the shower. She smells of one of those days that's just the perfect amount of humid. Skin dappled in drops. I want to bury my head in her neck and inhale this, commit this to a sense memory that will never fade.

And, after, exhausted, padding to grab water for her, I can smell her on me. Not on me, in me, permeating me.

Handing her the glass, I look at her, at every exquisite inch of her bathed in muted cyan from the moon and it's then I realize

I can't resist her anymore than
the waves can resist crashing against the shore.

"What?"

"Nothing", I kiss away her question. I don't want her to know that I'm drowning in her and I don't want to be saved.

My Heart Dances

This woman
shakes my soul
like no other.
I vibrate
to the rhythm
of her heartbeat.
She calls the tune
with a smile.
My heart dances.

IN THE GRASS

You're everything
I've ever wanted
And, nothing I don't need.

Let's lay our backs
in the wet grass
and let our hearts
just bleed.

I HEART NEW YORK

She is feisty.
She is gorgeous.
She is bright lights at night.
She is one lone saxophone.
She is sirens wailing.
She is wet streets at dawn.
She is the smell of warm bread in the cold morning.
She is hot jazz and punk rock.
She is tough as nails.
She is soft as steam from a grate.
She is late night coffee.
She is a wild haired brunette with her arms and heart
stretched as wide as the skyline.
She is a Midwestern schoolboy's dream.
She is New York.
She is home.

INSATIABLE

I crave you
Like hunger
Like thirst
Like madness
And, nothing
Will sate or slake
Or, make me sane
But you.

Favorite

Diffuse light holding your curves in a delicate
chiaroscuro.

The tender valley just below your hip bone, my fingers
just tucked below lace.

Your neck as it dovetails into the shoulder, the pool
between it and your collar bone.

Above your heart, my heart, gleaming bright in the
glow of morning.

The slope rising from your lower back down to where it
disappears into your leg, beckoning me with your
smooth warm silk skin.

A smile breaking across your cheeks, eyes, glorious
mouth.

Dark spun satin smoke framing deep soulful eyes that
crackle with mischief, promise.

But, if I had to pick a favorite thing on you...

It would be my hands.

TAKE HER

Ravage her
Devour her
Take her
Every part
Bend her to
Your every whim
But never
Break her heart

LOSE YOURSELF

Plan on losing
your dress,
panties,
breath,
decorum,
control,
sense of time,
reason,
ability to form words,
mind
and heart
in my hands.

DETAILS

The way her rich silk skin dips into the pool above her
collar bone.

That soft pad just below her hip bone.

The little V that her front teeth make when she smiles
broadly.

The bright flecks she swears aren't there in her ordinary
eyes.

The change in those same eyes and her breathing when
I tell her exactly what she's thinking.

Her fingers between her impossible lips.

My name on her tongue, whispered like a lightning
crack, standing my hair on end.

Her favorite part of me on my favorite part of her.

Her soft purr across my skin, tucked safely into my
arms wrapped around her, my lips on her hairline.
Hearts, breathing keeping time together.

The way she shines like I've somehow looked through a
veil between worlds and found an angel who secretly
wished to be human.

BOOKSTORE

Hunt you through the stacks of the old bookstore, a rare
volume I can't wait to get my hands on, the scent of
your leaves haunts my fingers.

WRITE HER

The girl lounges tangled in sheets as the boy lazily traces loops on her skin with his finger.

"What are you writing?" she asks.

"Mine."

SHE IS...

She is both my madness and my sanity.

She is the calm quiet eye of my storm.

She is the whisper in the maddening din.

She is a rare mix of dirty mind, exquisite beauty, curves
that make your hands ache, deep heart and mischief that
you want for your own.

She is peace in the shape of a woman.

ERATO

Muse of my words,
she pours them
into my mind,
filtered through
the flames of my heart
and written in fire
to burn
half as bright as she.

No More Words

Words cannot compare
to breathing the same air;
the curve of hips
and bitten lips,
hands buried in her hair.

THE SAFEST DANGER

My palm
across her throat,
her warmth,
her pulse beneath.
Eyes narrow.
Breathing slows.
She trusts
I'm the safest danger
she's ever known.

This is the Moment

She's burned this moment into the heart of me. I smell us in the room. The air shakes with possibility. All I want is this feeling forever.

Barely there in the dim light shimmers a silver circle against black leather and her pale silk skin, lips apart, her hand on her heart.

She's exhausted, breathless, spent. You wrap her tightly in your arms, stroking her skin as her breath, heart rate slowly synchs with yours.

She exhales against your chest, ripples across your skin. You kiss her forehead, taste the sweet salt of her. So much beauty your eyes well.

Both your battered hearts throb in unison. Lounging in the doorway between sleep and wake, you hover, weightless in the dim light, sublime.

This is why we're here. This is why we existed this long to find each other. This is the connection. This is the moment of everything.

DIRTY

Taint my mind
with the dirty of yours.
Make my
unclean thoughts
move my
thick rough peasant paws.
Squeal your way
into my ragged heart.

Let's Begin

Arms looped through hers from behind, hands clasp her
wrists, my teeth on the slope between neck and
shoulder, her thighs tremble in bliss.

By rise and fall of her breasts
I hear her sighs deepen and slow,
as my hand slips
from its home on her hip
to explore her valley below.

WELCOME

Your body
Whispered to my hands
The first time they met
"Welcome home."

POSSESSION

Ruin her.
Possess her utterly.
Mind. Body. Heart.
Down to her fucking marrow.
Until the softness
of her skin on skin
whispers your name.

SHE SEES ME

She sees me.
Even when I'm not there.
Even when I don't see myself.
Even when I hate what I see.
She sees me.
For me.
For us.

SUNRISE

She is a sunrise
over the Aegean.
She is a sunset
over the Pacific.
She is swaying gently
to soft music.
clothed in only moonlight
She is a gentle snowfall
outside a warm kitchen
clutched around coffee
and stolen long looks.
She is tangled sheets and hair and hands and hearts.
She is moments of beauty
that shake your soul
and say,
"Remember this.
This is Important.
This is everything right here."

TAKE YOU

I'll take you to the very edge.
Beg met to send you over.
Float you softly down
to my waiting arms.
Make you feel
cherished,
desired,
loved,
safe.

BOOKSTORE #2

Used bookstore.
Your back against the stacks.
Skirt hiked.
Panties pushed aside.
You wet my fingers
as I turn your pages
and read your mind.

INKED

I will teach you
To write
In ink indelible
These words
That will never fade
From your heart
I. Am. His.

RAISE

I may raise
your wrists above your head
your skirt hem
your heart rate
and, marks upon your skin
but, never

my voice.

DEVIL

The devil on her shoulder
is in love with her
beyond words, hope;
just happy to be
close enough
to her heart
to dance
to the beat of it.

The Girl You Knew

I want to put laugh lines around your eyes and smile
lines around your mouth from snickering at the
incredibly filthy things I whisper in your ear.

Wind your slowly silvering hair around my finger as it
glows incandescent in the sloping sun. Grin the girl you
knew in you to the surface.

CONTENTS

I would pour out
the contents
of my heart
and set it all aflame,
just to hear
her impossible mouth
slowly moan
my name.

MEROPE #3

Like Orion,
I would chase her
across the sky
for eternity
if it meant
that I might run
in the spark shower wake
of her stardust.

SIE IST...

Sie ist meine Augen.
Sie ist meine Herz.
Sie ist meine Lieb.
Sie ist meine Schmerz.

FUCK LOVE

Fuck Love.

Give me whatever this is.

This beautiful pain
that ceases
with a look in her eye,
the touch of her skin.

Kill me with this knife.

DESCANT

She is the bright descant
to my melancholy melody,
a bird on the roadside slipstream
matching pace with
my rising, falling hand.

HARVEST

She runs through the wheat field of my mind caressing
the tops with her soft hands that every last grain bears
the taste of her.

Not the Birds

Not the birds crooning in the stand of bamboo.
Not the sirens wailing down 7th.
Not the rumble of the trash truck in the alley.
Not the city shaking itself awake.
Nothing can drown out the throb of my heart,
the babble of blood in my ears,
the music my soul plays,
when I wake up next to you.

WILD HAIRED GIRL #2

Knee socks.
silken thighs,
cardigan,
smoldering eyes,
wild black hair.
breathy sighs;
her fierce beauty,
my demise.

MINDREADER

She reads my thoughts, which skitter across my grey
eyes like sparks. She brightens, giddy at the sweet danger
she sees there.

STEAM

Warming my fingers by burying them in her hair and clenching them; her gasp steaming from her lips as I catch it with my hungry mouth.

WORDS FAIL

Palm to palm, fingers laced.
I feel her pulse in mine.
Our eyes fill the silence.
Just us.
Just being.
Time stops.
Words fail.
Peace.

WHERE I BELONG

Palm on the curve of her hip, fingers tucked under the edge of her panties on the soft well below the hip bone.

Where my hand belongs.

The spot between the soft upper part inside her thigh and her beautiful orchid, where taut muscle travels between.

Where my teeth belong.

The delicate rise from her lower back, arching soft flesh down to where it cascades into her beautiful thighs.

Where my marks belong.

PLAYGROUND GIRL

She is the girl
lazily swinging,
feet bare
her black tendrils
smoke in the breeze,
dress clinging
for dear life
in the playground
of my head.

MY WORDS ARE HER

Every word I write is hers.
My fingers trace her name
spelled a thousand ways. Thoughts
in the shape of words
in the shape of her.

LATE SUMMER

She smiles into the ocean breeze, wild hair swirling;
sundress waves like sheers in an open window I long to
climb through.

MY FAVORITE READ

Every move,
every sigh,
every moan;
everything
you do
for me
is poetry
from your soul
to mine.
You are
my favorite read.

Light

She sees me as I am.
My darkness flickers
as she takes it,
every last bit,
and replaces it
with the light
in her eyes.

FRESHLY SHOWERED GIRL

Her skin steams,
shower fresh,
hair gleams,
a spill of ringlets,
her eyes, lips, shimmer.

And, all I can think
is how I can dirty her.

I BELIEVE

Her eyes
Her body
Her heart
Makes me believe
In magic
In destiny
In myself

SUNLIGHT

Diffuse orange sunlight whispering its arrival through
the sheers into the blue shadows of the room; her
tanned curves like sleepy dunes disappear under grass
green bed clothes. Her eyes, lit by this transitory light,
flash like tiger jasper or onyx with each turn of her head.
A pale chiaroscuro plays with her frame, reverently
lighting on her skin like my fingertips.

Her lids still heavy with sleep slip into slow motion. A
smile spreads across her face as the sun and her eyes
catch fire.

She looks at me, away from the sunrise stretching it's
arms across the sky, she looks at me and suddenly I
can't hear anything but the sound of my own heart
pounding her name.

NOTES

Her pulse in my palm
across her elegant throat
is the loveliest melody
God ever wrote.
Her eyes smile fire
as I savor each note.

DIVER DOWN

I will fall
into the depths
of your heart
forever
and
never
reach
the bottom.

MAN IN HER MIRROR

When I look in the mirror, I see:
A heart full of scars
A flaws I can't hide
A disappointment
in eyes I can look into
When she looks at me, I see:
A heart she holds dear
A strength I can't hide
A wealth of possibilities
in eyes she can't stop looking into
I want to be the man in her mirror

MY/HER

My arms
Her armor
My words
Her book
My safe
Her haven
My unravel
Her look

OASIS

Hair an explosion of smoke.
Eyes of campfire embers.
Mouth made of fire.
Hips of warm sleepy dunes
slope to an oasis
where I quench my thirst.

Symphony

The feel of her in my hands.
The notes she sings when I play her.
Or, even the silent looks
scored with shallow breath.
She is my symphony.

GROWL

My fists in your wild black hair,
that beautiful, sinful mouth
full of me,
intoxicating eyes
locked on mine,
as I growl
down your throat.

LEFT

She left her:
Scent on my sheets.
Taste on my lips.
Light in my dark.

And, took my:
Breath in her lungs.
Marks on her skin.
Heart in her hands.

HALF

I am not half. Neither is she. We are both whole people. But, there's this magic that happens when we are together. Each whole becomes half of a new thing. Us.

That's not the magic. The magic is that each whole person makes the other more whole.

She feels more beautiful, desired, confident. Because she is.

I feel more interesting, desired, at peace. Because I am.

Our halves make us whole, without reducing either.

And, in this way, I'm fairly certain love defies the laws of physics.

END

I broke my own heart to let you out.

MORE

A heart
made of china
lies broken
on the floor
yet every jagged
puzzle piece
softly whispers
"More".

OWN THE MOON

Try to
hold her
through the
ebb and flow
of her
rough tide
and monsoon.

Try to
see her
through the
brilliant glow
of her
dark eyes
and not swoon.

Try to
win her
though you
foolishly
claim her
you cannot
own the moon.

EXILED

I dream of her skin
underneath my hand
like an exile
aches
for his own homeland.

SQUARED CIRCLE

We fight for love
Each other
Ourselves
But, the real opponent is fear
Fear of never enough
Fear of what if instead
Fear of why me
Fear of her heart
Fearing his
Bed like a boxing ring
Each night
Exhausted, spent
On our backs
And, when the bell rings
we realize it's a draw
And, we've both lost.

I AM HER HEARTBREAK

I am her heartbreak at night.
I am her tears come the dawn.
I am her all that was right,
now turned horrible wrong.
I took her happy away,
replaced with an ache so strong.
I made her regret the day
she played me her favorite song.

SADNESS

I put the sadness in her eyes and I can't take it out.

I have broken the words that mean the most to me, the most to her.

Cut myself on the shards of each letter; bleeding ink from my veins.

WORDS LIKE BROKEN GLASS

My words
were all I had
to touch her with
now each caress
an unkind cut
raising
yet another scar
on the
soft flesh
of her broken heart.

NO RETURN

My heart won't return to me.
I've broken it too many times.
She can keep it forever.
She took better care of it
than I ever did.

Beyond Words

I adored her
beyond words
and now
that's all I have left of her.

Memories Like Ghosts

Bright memories
fade
into dull pain
like fresh ghosts
unaware
they're dead.

I MISS YOU

I miss you.
I miss the me you make me.
I miss the we you and I made.
I miss the way your skin fits my hands.
I miss the way your eyes fire at my grin.
I miss the soft dawn whispers
holding your warmth close
and your lips closer.
I miss the hundred sundry sublime moments
that you have given me.
I miss it all.
I miss everything.
I miss us.

PHOTOGRAPHIC MEMORY

Time
slices memory
into photographs
of your life.

Keep those albums safe
for, sometimes,
they're all we have left
from the fire.

SIREN

Swimming
toward the grey dawn
through the crashing tide
of dreams of her,
praying
for the undertow
to keep me, drown me
in her siren's arms.

TRUST FALL

Without trust
there is no love.

Trust is the air
love breathes.

I AM THE CRACKS IN HER HEART

Searching
the ruins of us
for the weakness
that made it fall.

Catching
a glimpse of me
in the broken mirror
of her eyes
and have my answer.

HANDHOLD

It hurts to breathe
when we crush our hearts
in each other's hands.

But, it's the only handhold
we still have on us.

My Heart Knows Her Name

Break my fingers so I cannot write.
Cut my tongue so I cannot speak.
Drown my mind so I cannot think.
My heart will still sing your name.

FAERIETALE ENDING #2

Fighting his dragons
to be her lord
with a cracked shield
and a broken sword.
Aches for his good name
to be restored.
She, his homeland
he longs to explore.

IN THE CORNER

I've painted myself into the corner. I curse my own stupidity, procrastination, and lack of forward thinking. I have to wait for this paint to dry so I can exit, leaving behind only an unfinished part roughly the size and shape of me.

Sure, I could paint it now the best I could but it wouldn't quite be perfect except as a perfect reminder of how imperfect I am; like a faint scar on a beautiful heart for which you are truly, truly sorry.

ADRIFT

If I could cast the fearful heavy words overboard, right our boat to our course I would. I am adrift alone in rough seas, no land in sight.

Unmoored in a sea of doubt. Mistakes of my past, the leaden albatross dragging me down through salt water tears.

I ache to take her ache away. Tether her to me and brave the storm together. In her eyes, the howl subsides. In her arms is calm.

MISSING

My hands
miss her skin.
My mouth
her taste of sin.
My eyes
her mischief grin.
My heart
which let her in.

CONFLAGRATION

The dark ember of one lie sets fire to reams of truth; the smoke choking you as their grey ashes float like dust to cover every surface in your soul in the memory of her.

SCARS

Scars
have an echo
your words,
your actions
can never drown out.

CHOKE

Choke
me to death
with the hands
of the man
who hurt you.

HOUSEGUEST

Dreams of
a future past
seep from my veins
like a guest
who has overstayed
their welcome.

THE PRICE

He knows
full well
what her pain
will cost.

The map
to her treasure
which he
has lost.

THE DEVIL #2

Lucifer,
he never stopped
being an angel.

And, God,
she never stopped
loving him.

FIX US

Even when
she says she hates me,
I can see in
through her eyes
down to her soul
and I hear her heart whisper,
"I love you. Fix us."

WHOLEHEARTEDLY

I wish
her heart
whole.

With
or without
me in it.

Departure

The boy sighs as images of the girl dissipate. Light
knifes through the blinds, cuts his eyes open to the grey
ache of dawn.

She shuts the door behind her. Its latch click reminds
the boy of a bucket down a well, her fading footsteps of
axes felling cherry trees.

TUNED

My entirety still vibrates to her frequency.

A tuning fork involuntarily singing one sorrowful note
after her touch is gone.

BURN THIS

Her tears
in the shape of words
writing a library of sorrow
page by page
book by book
I weep for a match
to burn it all
and me with it.

HEART IS A MUSCLE

Stiletto toes akimbo like a knife fight. Taut calves, thighs rise to a pencil skirt clinging to thick hips like a desperate lover, fiercely.

Her hand on her hip frames a tight cardigan, its tensile strength tested by the sheer her of her. Above it, a smile like lightning flashes.

Mischief in her cigarette coal eyes, hair like black smoke. The kind of woman you already know is going to leave a scar that won't fade.

But, you're like, "Fuck it. My heart can take it." And, it can.

And, it does. And, it hurts but you knew it would be worth it.

And, it was.

Because your heart is a muscle, not bone. It bruises, sometimes deeply, but it doesn't break. It keeps on beating until it no longer can.

WE ARE STARDUST

We are stardust.
We are dirt.
We are love.
We are hurt.
We are nothing.
We are all.
We are fools
who took the fall.

EVERYWHERE

Everywhere I look is some remnant of you layered upon
the world like sheer in a window where you stand on the
balcony waiting for me.

Your head turned, eyes cast back over your shoulder,
beckoning with their curled finger gaze. Your hair
taunting the breeze to come play.

And, in this sweet torture ache of liminality, music and
images spin their web around my head, blind and deaf to
anyone but you.

LUCKY

Love will rip your heart out
and show it to you
before you die
and, if you're lucky,
you will love
every fucking minute of it.

Torchbearer

I will carry
this torch
for her
she lit
with her smile
fanned with her laugh
until my fingers burn
like the memory
of her skin.

SOMEWHEN

She has my heart
with her it'll stay.
I'll never regret
giving it away.
No more words.
Nothing left to say.
Maybe there will be;
somewhen, someway.

CODA

Just when you think the music is over, there's a coda; a chance to see it to its rightful conclusion.

ALTERNATE ENDING

Help me
write us
a new ending
to the best story
I've ever read.

A ME WORTH YOU

Whatever becomes of us
I'm glad you happened to me.

Because you made me realize
there was a me worth you
inside of me.

YOUR NAME ON MY HEART

My heart is your to hold.
And, the treasures yours alone.
Remember that when
I am not near.
Always, all ways.

THE ME SHE SEES

The me she sees
the one I see reflected in her eyes
when she looks at me.,
The me before the scars
but somehow wiser for them,
the me before the pain
but richer for having survived;
the me she sees in me.
And, like some secret alchemy,
I am the me I was
and the me I long to me.

LAST RITES

Let the last breath in my lungs be in praise of your beauty.

Let the last light in my eyes belong to you.

ABOUT THE AUTHOR

KIRK DIEDRICH is originally from Detroit.
He currently lives in Los Angeles
with his dog, Karma.

www.ingramcontent.com/pod-product-compliance
Lightning Source LLC
Chambersburg PA
CBHW022114040426
42450CB00006B/703